THE REFORMED PANTSER'S GUIDE TO PLOTTING

MAPPING OUT YOUR BOOK CHAPTER BY CHAPTER

ABIGAIL DRAKE

ALSO BY ABIGAIL DRAKE

Women's Fiction
The South Side Stories
The Dragonsong Law Offices
The Hocus Pocus Magic Shop
The Enchanted Garden Cafe
Passports and Promises
Delayed Departure
Sophie and Jake
Saying Goodbye
The Tink Holly Chronicles
Rebel Without a Claus
Other
Love, Chocolate, and a Dog Named Al Capone
Lola Flannigan
Traveller
Young Adult Fiction
The Bodyguard
Starr Valentine
Tiger Lily

For more about Abigail, visit her website:
https://abigaildrake.com

For all the struggling pantsers out there.

FOREWORD

Dear Writer,

Is your middle saggy? Does your ending seem weak? Has someone told you that your main character is perhaps (gasp) unlikable? Does your plot have more holes than Swiss cheese?

Never fear. No book is unfixable—not even yours! You just need a handy dandy, step-by-step method to analyze the structure of your story and figure out where you went wrong.

That is the purpose of this book. It's a simple way of mapping out your story and making it more appealing to readers. It doesn't matter if you've already written your novel or if you're just starting out. There are certain key elements you need to incorporate if you want your work to go from "meh" to "marvelous."

How do I know this?

Because I've been there. My first book sucked—big time. My second one sucked slightly less. But it wasn't until I wrote a YA sci-fi romance called *Starr Valentine,* that everything fell into place.

Starr Valentine was my third book, but I still had no idea what I was doing. I wrote that novel in ten weeks. My edit was running a spell check and doing a single reread of my manuscript. I had no critique partners or beta readers. I did it all wrong, and yet somehow signed with my first agent four days after I began submitting it. It took me years to figure out how I got so lucky with this book, but the answer was really quite simple.

Starr Valentine started as a short story that won a prize in a sci-fi contest. Because I had the short story to use as a template, turning it into a full-length novel wasn't hard. In fact, it was kind of fun. A proud pantser, I was plotting and didn't even realize it.

For those who might not know that term, a pantser is a magical creature who sits down at a desk and writes without actually knowing what will happen next in the story. Pantsers think it's better that way because there is nothing more interesting than being surprised and amazed by what occurs in your own book.

On the other hand, a plotter works diligently to plot out a book before they even begin writing it. These are the people who like outlines and structure. They prefer order over chaos.

Pantsers *are* chaos, but there is no right or wrong way. You should do what works best for you but try to be realistic and, most importantly, flexible. You don't have to be hard-core one way or the other. It's okay to be a combo of the two. You aren't cheating on the pantser side of your nature if you plot, and you're not letting things get entirely out of hand if you pants (not a verb, but too bad).

If you're a plotter, you'll spend more time before you start writing because you'll need to think things through. If you're a pantser, you'll spend more time at the end trying to fix what you may have missed. Both take roughly the same number of hours, but which one is less frustrating? And how can you learn to write a book that will finally hit the mark?

Hitting the mark is the tricky part. No one tells you that, but it's true. It's like finding the sweet spot on the racquet in tennis. There is nothing more satisfying.

Have you ever experienced that feeling when the thoughts are flowing so quickly you almost can't type fast enough to keep up? When the words come to you, and you get so immersed in them you forget everything else?

It's a great feeling, and it's what I experienced with *Starr Valentine*, but let me be straight here. I had a great time writing that book and success in finding an agent quickly, but it was luck, not skill, that got me there. I hit the right person at the right time with the right story.

Piiiing.

The sweet spot on the racquet. But the rest of the process ended up being a whole lot more challenging.

Even though my agent tried hard to sell my book, sadly no one was particularly interested in purchasing it. Eventually, I parted ways with that agent and sold the book to a small press on my own, but this entire experience was definitely a wake-up call.

All along, I'd felt something was wrong with my book, but I couldn't put my finger on it. As my agent submitted it and publisher after publisher rejected it, several things became clear, but one thing stood out more than all the others.

Many of the people who read my book didn't immediately like the main character. I heard it from different editors and in different ways, but the problem was clear. They didn't connect with my protagonist. They weren't rooting for her. They didn't care if she succeeded or failed.

"Wait," I'd wanted to explain. "She's only unlikable *at first*. By the end you will love her."

Unfortunately, they never got to the end. Most of them probably never got past the first chapter. I basically doomed myself from page one.

Having an unlikable main character was not the only issue with my book in its original form—it was just the first thing that stood out. The book could have been fixed so easily, but because I didn't understand what was wrong at the time, the whole process became frustrating.

I kept writing, though, and I kept learning. It took several years, and about sixteen additional books, before things finally clicked into place. For some writers, it clicks right away. For others, it never happens. This book is for the non-clickers, for the writers struggling to figure out where they went off the rails and how to get back on track. Or for those just starting out who have no idea which way to go.

I want to be very clear—there is nothing wrong with being a pantser. There is also nothing wrong with being a plotter. Many writers are a mix of both, and that's okay, too. But when I began writing my seventeenth book, I found myself flailing, and decided to do something crazy. I'd read a million books on plotting. Why not compile all the information garnered from some very smart people and put it together into a useable system?

Spoiler alert: It worked.

After writing one book successfully using this method, I decided to teach a workshop on the subject. Putting the whole thing together in a cohesive manner was harder than

I anticipated, but the results paid off. A few days after the workshop, one of the writers in attendance told me she went home after taking my class and finally fixed a book she'd been working on for ten years.

Ten years.

That's why I decided to compile what I'd learned on the subject and make that workshop into a book. If it helped one writer, I thought maybe it could help someone else, too. This information comes from years of trial and error, from listening to other writers, and from reading books on plotting. I also took tons of classes, both at conferences and in webinars, to find what worked best, but every writer is different. Every book is different. What works for you with one book might not work on another. Take what you like from this system and discard the rest. I'm not here to tell you what to do (although I can be a little on the bossy side at times). I'm here to help you figure out how to do it your way.

So, what *is* your way?

I'm guessing if you're reading this, you're a pantser, but this system will work for plotters, too. Either way, I promise not to waste your time. You should be writing, not reading, so I'll try to make this fast, fun, and easy. There is, however, one crucial thing you need to know.

A lot of pantsers think plotting will kill their creativity. It does not have to be that way. They also believe it will make their work tedious and formulaic. It doesn't have to be that way, either. To prove it, I'm going to use examples throughout this book from several diverse novels and movies most of us know and love: *Harry Potter and the Sorcerer's Stone, The Hunger Games, Legally Blonde*, and everyone's favorite Christmas movie, *Die Hard*.

If you haven't seen at least one of these movies (or read

one of the books), I recommend you do so before you get started. It'll make so much more sense to you if you're familiar with these stories. Also, you'll catch a bunch of cultural references you may have missed in the past. It's a win-win all around.

These are all very different stories. *Harry Potter and the Sorcerer's Stone* is a middle-grade fantasy, and *The Hunger Games* is a young adult dystopian. *Legally Blonde* is a comedy, but if it were a book, I'd say it nicely straddles the line between women's fiction and rom-com. And *Die Hard* (besides being the most excellent Christmas movie ever next to *Elf*) is an action movie.

Since all four work with this chapter-by-chapter plotting structure, I think it kills the myth that plotting makes you predictable. Your story will be original no matter what. Don't use predictability as an excuse because you're scared about plotting. There is nothing to be afraid of because I promise I'll hold your hand and guide you through the whole process.

Note: You might disagree with some of my conclusions regarding where the plot points hit exactly in each of these stories. No problem. I will not be offended if you think I'm wrong, because there is a lot open to interpretation. The point is, when you peel away the extra layers, these books and movies all follow a similar structure.

This method is a template. You do not have to follow it precisely. For example, you may want to combine what I have listed for Chapters One and Two into one chapter, or you may need to make what I have written as Chapter Nine into several chapters.

That's okay. You are driving this bus. It's only going to crash if you let it.

This analogy is not a hidden way of saying, "Stay in your lane."

No. No way. Don't stay in your lane.

Swerve a little and see what happens, or maybe take an alternate route to your destination. Just stay on the road. You might be pleasantly surprised where you end up.

1

SOMETHING HAPPENS

A ct I. Scene I. Your story begins.
Someone once told me the first paragraph is the most valuable real estate in your book. I agree with that, and I'll even go so far as to say the first few pages will make or break your novel.

Why?

Because if you don't do it properly, your reader will stop reading. I've heard agents and editors say they knew after reading the first two pages whether the story would be compelling enough to continue or not. One agent told me she knew after reading only one page. No pressure, but I'm not exaggerating. It's important.

To help you remember the purpose of each chapter, I'm using super obvious phrases as chapter headings. For chapter one?

SOMETHING HAPPENS.

Please don't say "duh." I know you're thinking it. But lots of writers really do start at the wrong place. After you've messed up a few times, you kind of figure out where the right place is, which is when (drum roll) SOME-

THING HAPPENS. And by that, I mean when something unexpected occurs—an inciting incident or a catalyst.

I'm going to spend a lot of time on Chapter One because it is so important. There are certain key elements you need to have in this chapter, no matter the genre.

What are these elements?

1. A GREAT HOOK

The hook is the first sentence and the first words your reader will get from you. Make those words unforgettable.

"It was a dark and stormy night" worked for Madeleine L'Engle when she penned *A Wrinkle in Time*, but the millions of other people who attempted to use the same phrase in their books? It didn't work out quite as nicely for them.

Was it actually a dark and stormy night? Maybe it was, and that's great, but don't start your book with a sentence about the weather. Any weather. Dark, stormy, rainy, sunny, hot, cold, frigid, or *il fait un temps nuageux* (my favorite weather response in high school French). It doesn't matter. Even if you sound super sophisticated and cool by saying "*nuageux*" instead of cloudy, it's unimportant. Unless you're writing a book in which the weather plays a critical role and is central to the plot, please don't do it. Trust me on this.

And watch out for other clichés as well, like starting your book as your character is waking up, looking in the mirror, and noticing their physical attributes. You can describe your character's flowing locks, sparkling eyes, and voluptuous curves in a better and more creative way later. The mirror thing has been done—a lot. Don't be the writer to do it again.

Oh, and if the hook ends up being part of a crazy dream, even worse. Unless you want your readers (especially agents and editors) to turn away from your manuscript, avoid the crazy dream trope. They have read it many, many times before. You want your hook to be exciting and new, to pull your reader into the story from the first sentence. You want to hook them as they've never been hooked before.

That sounded weird, but you get my drift. Make the hook as intriguing and original as you possibly can, and you will not regret it. Promise.

2. OPENING IMAGE

The opening image is a visual that represents key elements and gives the reader insight into the heart of the story. It must have power and impact, and it should mean something significant. It's a snapshot of the main character's daily life (and possibly their problem) before the adventure commences.

Examples of solid opening images:

A. Harry Potter living in the cupboard under the stairs.

B. Katniss Everdeen hunting in the forest with her bow and arrow.

C. Elle Woods getting ready for her big date with her boyfriend, Warner.

D. John McClane clutching his armrest on the plane as he lands in LA.

Note: You could also say the opening image in *Harry Potter and the Sorcerer's Stone* happens in the prologue, when the wizarding world is introduced, along with McGonagall, Dumbledore, Hagrid, and the little, orphaned baby, Harry. It's a great opening, but nothing is quite as poignant as the image of poor Harry living under the stairs. It gets you right in the feels.

3. SETUP

The setup occurs when you expand on the "before" snapshot of the opening image. Your character's life might be great (like Elle's) or awful (like Harry's and Katniss's), but it doesn't matter. No matter how wonderful your protagonist's life might be, there has to be something missing. Something significant. Your job here is to present the main character's world and hint at what that missing part is —even if the character doesn't fully grasp it themselves.

Sneaky, huh? It's actually super mega-sneaky because your reader can't know what's missing either—not in any great detail, at least. Even if you do give them a wink and a nod and point them in the right direction.

Another way to look at it—if the opening image is an Instagram post, the setup is a TikTok video (and I'm so uncool, I originally spelled that as "TickTock" and had to correct it, but you get my point).

How does this fit with our examples?

In *Harry Potter*, it's when Dudley is celebrating his birthday, and we get a clear picture of how the Dursleys mistreat Harry and the differences between Dudley's life and Harry's life. As if living under the stairs wasn't bad enough, he's given old socks as a gift and only plays with broken, discarded toys. It sucks.

In *The Hunger Games*, we learn poor Katniss has an emotionally absent mom and sweet little sister. Her family struggles to survive, and most of the weight rests on Katniss's shoulders. Like Harry, her life also sucks.

Elle Woods's life does not suck. It's completely different from Harry's or Katniss's. In the setup for *Legally Blonde*, it's a perfect, sunny, beautiful day in California, and Elle's world is sunny and perfect, too. She's wealthy, attractive, and popular. All her sorority sisters love her, and they're thrilled because they think she's about to be engaged to her soulmate Warner. Life is darned good for Elle Woods. No squirrel hunting for her, and definitely no hand-me-down socks.

In *Die Hard*, John's life isn't as great as Elle's, but it's certainly not as bad as Harry's or Katniss's. John's world, his new "normal," revolves around the status of his marriage. He and his wife Holly are separated. They live across the country from each other, and his children live with her. It's easy to see why he's unhappy. He wants his wife and family back but isn't exactly sure how to go about it. He's kind of a sad mess, and you see it right away—despite the mischievous smile playing on his lips and the twinkle in his eye.

That smile and twinkle go a long way in making John McClane both likable and appealing. Bruce Willis nailed it. That man is the master of the cheeky smirk.

4. THEME STATED

This usually happens during the setup, and the theme is the essence of your story. It's what your book is all about at its core. It's the message of the book, and it involves an essential truth about the main character. Usually, this truth is spoken to the protagonist or in their presence, but they don't understand it...not yet at least. They need to learn and grow and change in order to have the personal experience and context to embrace it fully.

When is the theme stated in our four example stories? You can argue the point, but in the case of *Harry Potter*, I think the theme is stated in the prologue when Dumbledore is speaking to McGonagall, and Hagrid brings the poor lightning-scarred baby Harry to leave him on the doorstep of the Dursley's house. Dumbledore mentions how Harry will not know his own importance, even while people all over the wizarding world are raising their glasses to "the boy who lived." That is key because it encompasses many of the themes in the book and the series: love, sacrifice, humility, family—to name a few.

In *The Hunger Games*, the theme is stated when Gale and Katniss discuss running away but know they can't. Their families wouldn't survive without them. That connects to quite a few of the book's themes: family, survival, poverty, hunger, injustice, etc.

In *Legally Blonde*, there are many options to choose from. I think one of the main themes is that people may underestimate Elle, but she is confident and believes in herself. That is shown in a scene when Elle is shopping, and a snarky employee tries to trick her into buying a dress. The employee says, "There's nothing I love more than a dumb blonde with Daddy's plastic." But Elle proves she is much more intelligent than she looks.

The theme is stated in *Die Hard* when John is talking to Argyle, the limo driver. He admits his stubbornness in refusing to follow Holly to LA and reveals his disappointment that she's succeeding at her new job. His stubbornness is what tore them apart, but it's also what will keep them together because that dude refuses to give up (which will become obvious later in the movie). Stubbornness is one of John McClane's defining characteristics.

5. CATALYST

This is the moment when the life of your character changes completely. It's the phone call in the middle of the night or the surprise marriage proposal. It's getting fired from a job, being dumped by the love of your life, winning something, or losing everything. It can be whatever you decide, but after it happens, the "before" world is gone, and change is coming.

What are the catalysts in our examples? You may already know, but I'll point them out just in case:

A. In *Harry Potter*, it's when the first owl arrives at the Dursley's home with the invitation for Harry to go to Hogwarts.

B. In *The Hunger Games*, it's when Primrose, Katniss's sweet little sister, is chosen as a tribute in the reaping.

C. In *Legally Blonde*, as you probably guessed, it's when Warner breaks up with Elle.

D. And in *Die Hard*, it's when shots are fired at Nakatomi Plaza. That doesn't happen until a bit later when all the different story lines (John's, Holly's, and Hans's), have been established, but it's the catalyst because it's what changes everything.

6. SAVE THE CAT! ™ MOMENT

If you haven't read Blake Snyder's books, you need to grab them all. He invented this term and a Save the Cat! ™ moment is something the character does to gain your sympathy and make you root for them. It comes from the theory that even a bad person can evoke sympathy or a connection if they perform an act of kindness (like saving a cat) at the beginning of the book or movie.

Simple, huh? And yet so brilliant.

Harry and Katniss don't need a specific moment. They are already sympathetic characters (one is an orphan, and the other is practically an orphan). But when Harry frees the snake from the zoo, it's a moment where we see his empathy for another trapped creature. And when Katniss comforts her sister when Prim wakes from a nightmare, it demonstrates she's a caring, loving older sister. It's like icing on the sympathy cake.

Even Elle doesn't have an exact moment. We see it in the way her sorority sisters care for her. They're thrilled she's about to get engaged. They line up to spray her with perfume and breath freshener. They adore her, and you know there must be a reason for this. For all her fluff and blondness, Elle is kind (you see it in how she treats others), lovable (as demonstrated by how others treat her), and a good person. She doesn't deserve what happens to her.

For John McClane, his Save the Cat! ™ moment happens in the first scene, while he's still on the airplane. He stands up to remove something from the overhead bin, and his fellow passenger sees John has a gun. John tells him not to worry and explains he's a cop. As he says that, he removes a giant teddy bear from the overhead bin. He's a cop, but he's also a loving father. He's a tough guy, and he's also sweet and thoughtful. The teddy bear gives you the warm fuzzies, doesn't it? That's because when John pulls out the teddy bear, he's saving the cat. It's on purpose. The bear is not random.

Other moments: Aladdin offering his hard-earned crust of bread to an orphan. Cinderella saving Gus Gus from the mousetrap. Disney loves saving the cat. Everyone loves saving the cat, so do it, especially if you potentially have a character who is not immediately likable. You'll thank me (and the late Blake Snyder) for it later.

That's it for Chapter One. Is your brain sufficiently full? Do you hate me yet? Take heart, dear writer. The first chapter is the hardest part.

Well, kind of.

The good news is you only have nineteen chapters or so left to write.

Yay.

2
_____

A REACTION TO WHAT HAPPENS

I told you I was going to wow you with my chapter headings. Are you sufficiently wowed? Because Chapter Two is precisely what I'm calling it—a reaction to the catalyst in Chapter One.

Easy peasy, right?

Yes, and no. At this point in your book, there's a debate going on. It might be an actual debate, or it might be internal, but your protagonist is dealing with feelings of doubt and has many questions.

Can they face this challenge? Do they have what it takes? Do they even *want* to do this? Should they go on this journey at all?

Chapter Two isn't solely a debate and a reaction. It's also the last chance for the hero to chicken out.

In *Harry Potter*, the reaction to the catalyst doesn't come from Harry. It comes from his uncle. Mr. Dursley freaks out when those letters start arriving from Hogwarts. He is bound and determined to keep Harry from seeing them and goes so far as to board up the house to keep those letters out.

He and his wife have managed to hold the wizarding world at bay for nearly a decade. He's not going to stop now.

Katniss's reaction in *The Hunger Games* is immediate and visceral. As soon as Prim is chosen, Katniss volunteers as a tribute. You can see everything clearly expressed on Katniss's face in the movie—shock, horror, resignation, realization, and then the decision. It's obvious, without Katniss even saying a word, what's going on in her head. She knows she'll likely die if she enters the games, but she is *certain* Prim will die. And Katniss, being Katniss, is willing to sacrifice herself for her sister without a great deal of internal or external debate. It's the right thing to do, and she has no other option.

In *Legally Blonde*, Elle responds to the catalyst in a fairly predictable way. She gets depressed and eats chocolate. She doesn't want to leave her room, and her sorority sisters are getting worried. The normalness of Elle's chocolate-bingeing reaction to her breakup makes it both believable and compelling.

John's reaction in *Die Hard* is believable as well. He hears shots fired, sticks his head out of Holly's office, and recognizes several things at once. First of all, something terrible is going down. Secondly, his wife is in the middle of it. Thirdly, John knows if he confronts the terrorists now, he might make the situation worse. People, including Holly, could get hurt, and John would most likely die. Every fiber in his being tells him to go toward his wife, but his training and knowledge make him turn and go the other direction. He leaves now to save Holly and the other hostages later, but he is not happy about it.

Guess what? That's it for Chapter Two. I told you it was easy. And Chapter Three is only slightly more complicated.

3

TRYING TO PRETEND IT DIDN'T HAPPEN

A t this point in your story, your character might be a little scared and overwhelmed by what is going on. Even if "normal" wasn't great—even if it really, really sucked—at least your character knew what they were dealing with.

This chapter is about three things:

- Fear of change.
- Fear of failure.
- Doubt in their abilities.

Change is scary, and for a moment (or for many moments), the main character doubts they are doing the right thing. They figure the devil they know is better than the one they don't and decide to stick their head in the sand and do a fantastic imitation of an ostrich. They know the truth, but they aren't ready to face it yet.

In *Harry Potter*, it is once again Mr. Dursley who leads this parade. He takes the whole family to a remote, rocky island (on a dark and stormy night...but it's England, so that's typical there, and totally acceptable). Anyway, Mr. Dursley still thinks he can hide from the truth and from what is going to happen. Taking everyone to the island is his last attempt to keep things "normal."

There is always denial in this chapter, an effort to avoid the unavoidable. For Katniss, this moment occurs on the train when she refuses to talk to Peeta or seek advice and help from the only successful tribute from their district, Haymitch. Not that Haymitch is a great resource (he's a drunken mess), but Peeta is all about digging for advice. Katniss still isn't committed to playing the game.

Elle is committed—to getting into Harvard. She saw Warner's brother's engagement photo in the paper and noticed his fiancée (a girl "unfortunate" in the looks department) was also a student at Harvard Law. That prompts Elle to study for the LSAT with the help of her sorority sisters. Why is this a moment of denial? Because Elle sees getting into Harvard Law as a way back to Warner. She's still trying to go back to her old normal, and to Elle, that means being with Warner.

This is also the time when another theme in *Legally Blonde* arises. When he broke up with her, Warner said he wanted someone "serious." That is echoed when Elle's father says law school isn't for people like her—it's for "serious" people.

Elle's desire to become someone serious (aka intelligent and deserving of love and admiration) is a theme repeated throughout the movie. At one point Elle states it very clearly when she says, "Once Warner sees me as a serious law student, he'll want me back." Even she doesn't fully understand her own worth.

In *Die Hard*, John's moment comes when he understands he needs to call for help. He's not trying to pretend it didn't happen, but he's still hoping help will somehow come. The terrorists are in control, and he's torn about whether to step in or not. He doesn't want to make the situation worse and get Holly or anyone else killed. He's still in denial and trying to convince himself he won't have to step in and fix this on his own. His old normal is being a police officer, which means being part of a team, and following specific procedures. Going rogue is not part of his training, even if every part of him screams for him to do it to save his wife. But he can't. Not yet. He has to do things the "right" way first because it's been instilled in him.

Denial is more than just a river in Egypt.

Get it? The Nile. Denial. That's super funny, right?

Fine, it isn't super funny, but neither is denial. It's a frozen state, but it can't last forever in your book, which is why everything needs to change in the next chapter.

4

NO MORE PRETENDING

Ah, ignorance is bliss.

Well, not really. Ignorance is just ignorance, and it's time for your character to wake up and face reality. And it's also time for something very exciting to occur: Your first plot point.

What is a plot point?

It's an incident that directly impacts what will happen next in the story and changes the story's direction. It's something significant, something which will have a big impact on your character.

Do you know the saying, "When God shuts a door, he opens a window"? Kind of an insensitive way to deal with grief or loss, but in this case, it applies. The first plot point shuts a door, making it impossible for your character to go back, but it also opens a window—and your character must climb through that window in order to progress.

There can be significant events in your book that aren't plot points. The critical difference is the fact that a plot point moves the story forward, sometimes under duress. Often while your character is kicking and screaming. I liken it to trying to get a toddler out of a splash pad on a hot summer day. If you have kids, you know what I mean, but I have an even better analogy.

The plot is the bone structure of your book. Without bones, your body would be a floppy mess of skin and hair and blood and organs, right? Without a solid plot, your story is the same. And, if the plot is the skeletal structure of the book, the plot points are its ligaments. They hold the story together.

Think about a book you recently read. Try to remember which moments stood out to you. These are often the plot points. You were looking right at them and didn't even realize it! Silly you.

Why do you need to know this? Because plot points are the reason some stories are page-turners, and others make you yawn and shut the book. They might seem tiny and insignificant, but, like ligaments, your story would not stick together without them.

I once heard a simple description of why plot points are important. I cannot remember exactly where I heard it, so I can't give credit, but since it was useful, I'll share it here.

A great story usually reads something along the lines of "First this happened, *and so* this happened, *but then* this other thing happened, *which led directly to* this happening."

The importance is in how that sentence connects.

And so...

But then...

Which led to...

Those, my friend, are the plot points.

Without plot points, what do you have?

"This happened, and then this happened, and then this happened. The end."

Can you see the difference? It's like the toddler at the splash pad is telling the story.

"I was playing in the water, and then Mommy said it was time to go home, and then I cried, and then she made me leave."

But what is the same story from Mommy's point of view?

"We had a great day at the splash pad, *but* it was getting late, *and therefore* we had to leave *because* I needed to feed my rug rat dinner and get him to bed *in order for me to* be able to watch the exciting conclusion of *The Bachelorette* and drink wine with my besties."

Not an exciting story, perhaps, but a decent example. Without plot points, your story seems immature and under-developed. With plot points, your reader can easily under-stand the connection between events. And, in this example, you get to watch *The Bachelorette* and drink wine, too —bonus!

Back to all the plotting stuff—you may have already heard of something called the seven-point story structure. This system shows how the plot is connected using plot points and pinch points.

So, what is a pinch point?

It's when the character is under pressure (ouch, it pinches!) and must react to a plot point.

Let me give you a visual that is easy to remember. Have you ever seen photos of the Loch Ness Monster? The seven-point story structure makes me think of Nessie. First, you have the hook, and it's kind of like Nessie's tail. Her body rises to the first plot point—the part of Nessie you see above the water. The first pinch point is below the water. The midpoint is above the water. The second pinch point is below the water. The second plot point is above the water,

THE REFORMED PANTSER'S GUIDE TO PLOTTING

but the plot doesn't dip down again. It keeps going up until the climax, which is like Nessie's head. And, thanks to the wonders of Canva and Deposit Photos, I've created this graphic for you. Tada! Nessie the Plot Monster.

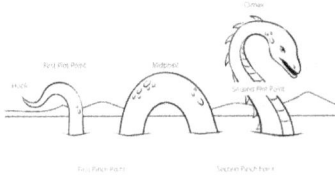

Why am I explaining all of this? And why am I creating Loch Ness Monster graphics? Don't worry. There is a reason. I want to make sure you understand the plot and pinch points to fully understand what needs to happen next, and I'm a visual learner. When I see it demonstrated like this, it makes sense to me, so I'm hoping it'll make sense to you.

Also, who doesn't like the Loch Ness Monster?

In Chapter Three, so much of the story truly starts. It's when your character realizes they have no choice. God has shut that door, and your character needs to find the window because something has happened that makes it impossible for them to continue to pretend everything is going to be okay. They may have hated their old normal, but even if they wanted to go back, it's no longer possible.

In *Harry Potter*, Hagrid arrives on that lonely rock of a miserable island, birthday cake in hand, and he informs Harry he is a wizard. For Harry, the door shutting on his old normal is a good thing, since his normal sucked, but he can't be sure yet. He doesn't know at this point what his new normal will be.

Katniss has an inkling her new normal will not be great since it'll be a bloody, violent fight to the death that she most likely will not survive. But she sees Haymitch, in all his drunken glory, and knows he survived, which changes everything. If he could do it, why can't she?

In *Legally Blonde*, the first plot point is a happy one. Elle gets into Harvard. Her hard work has paid off. But in *Die Hard*, it's the opposite. When John sees Mr. Takagi get murdered right in front of his eyes, he knows there is no going back. He also realizes Hans, the leader of the terrorists, is a bad, bad dude.

What happens next in your story? Don't ask me. It's up to your character to decide, and they'll do that in the next chapter.

5

MAKING A DECISION

I told you my chapter descriptors would be prosaic. The point is only to help you remember and understand without having to read through all my yammering to get to the heart of the matter. I'm hoping it will save you time in the long run, and I'm hoping this plotting method will save you time, too.

What happens in this chapter? As noted above (prosaically!), your character decides to act. By making this decision, they choose to break into Act II of the story. Act II will open with Chapter Six, but Act I is all about setup and rising action and reacting to events. It's short (in this example, it's only five chapters long). Act III is short, too. It's only four chapters long. Act II is the longest no matter what example you're using. It's the meat of the story, and it's where many writers get into trouble.

Have you ever heard of saggy middles? Those happen in Act II. No one ever talks about a saggy beginning or ending. The sagging all takes place in the middle of the story. If you've written a book already with a saggy middle, going through this plot map will help you figure out where the sag is and how to fix it. It's like a tummy tuck for your novel!

Because of this, Chapter Five, the last chapter in Act I, is essential. The main character makes a choice, and the journey commences. We leave the old world and enter the upside-down, opposite, unknown world of Act II. Often this involves an actual journey.

In *Harry Potter*, Hagrid has arrived and told Harry the truth about his origins: the famous "You're a wizard, Harry" line. That happened in Chapter Four. In Chapter Five, Harry decides to go with Hagrid. I don't think it was hard since the Dursleys are terrible people, but Harry takes a courageous step and agrees to leave behind what he knows and head off with a giant, hulking, and very hairy stranger. He chooses to act.

Katniss's decision to act almost coincides with her arrival at the Capitol. She demands Haymitch help them and stabs the table right between his fingers with a knife. She's not messing around. She has chosen to act, to fight, and to try to survive.

Elle is also on a journey. She's been accepted by Harvard and chooses to leave for Boston. An easy choice since Elle is very focused on her goal (aka Warner).

And John. Poor John. He's beating himself up for not saving Mr. Takagi, and he makes the decision to act. Since the phone lines have been cut (this was the '80s after all), he sets off the fire alarm. At first, it seems like it was a great idea. The firetrucks are coming—lights flashing and sirens wailing—and John is so happy. He stands at the window jumping up and down and grinning because he thinks that now everything will be okay! Salvation has arrived! His hopes, however, are soon dashed when he watches the firetrucks shut off their lights and turn around, going away from Nakatomi Plaza.

It's a big moment. All other options have been removed from the table. John will have to confront the terrorists on his own. Which he does right away—by killing one of the bad guys.

Phew. Grab some coffee. You're going to need it. It's time for Act II.

6

FRIENDS AND ENEMIES

Act II. Your story continues.

The second act opens with a bang, and it's time to have some fun with your book and your characters. They need allies. They need adversaries. And they need something else, as well.

The B story.

What is that exactly?

The B story, sometimes known as the subplot, can be many different things. It's often the part of your book when a romance pops up—unless you're writing a romance, of course. If that's the case, your love interest must be introduced right away. If you're writing a book that is not a romance, but has romantic elements or a romantic subplot, this is where you'd stick those things in.

Chapter Sex.

Oops. I mean Chapter Six.

By the way, since I write romance, I'm allowed to make those sorts of jokes. If you also write romance, I highly recommend a plotting book designed especially for romance writers. It's called *Romancing the Beat*, and it's by the fabulous Gwen Hayes. If you don't own this book, and you write love stories, buy it now.

But back to our B story. It does not have to be a romance. It can also be a "hate" story—like in the case of Harry and Draco, or a "best friends forever" story, like that of Harry, Ron, and Hermione.

The most important thing? You're introducing more characters and adding depth and interest to your story.

This is also when there's a discussion about the theme. It's the nugget of truth hinted at (or said outright) in the first chapter. Usually, this discussion is between the main character and the love interest, but it can also be with a best buddy or an arch-nemesis. The truth is out there, but your flawed character still doesn't get it yet.

The whole friends and enemies thing is shown quite nicely in *Harry Potter*. First, he goes to Diagon Alley to shop, an excellent intro to the wizarding world and many fabulous characters. Then he gets on the train and meets both Ron and Hermione. Lastly, he arrives at Hogwarts and has his first encounter with Draco.

It took J.K. Rowling several chapters to cover the whole friends and enemies thing, and you can do the same in your book. Don't feel forced to shove it all into one chapter. Like I mentioned before, this is a template; it's not carved in stone. You can add some chapters and delete others. Don't get hung up on fitting everything into neat little boxes. I mean, I like neat little boxes as much as the next gal (especially if they are small, blue, and come from Tiffany's), but allow yourself some flexibility. No Plot Police Officer is hovering over your shoulder as you type. You will not get a plotting ticket. I promise.

In *The Hunger Games*, Katniss is making friends in this chapter as well, her first one being Cinna, her stylist. But she's learning about her enemies, too—the other tributes, and most of them want to kill her. She's also getting closer to Peeta. Whether she likes it or not, they're becoming real friends.

Poor Elle isn't having much luck making friends at Harvard Law School. People shut her out. It's like she's landed on an alien planet, and she's not sure how to cope. Nothing seems to work. She finds out Warner is engaged, and his new fiancée, Vivian, isn't kind to Elle. Upset and crying, Elle drives off and ends up in a place that always makes her feel better—a salon. She meets Paulette, the woman who does her nails, and Elle finds a true friend in her new surroundings at last.

John McClane is not making friends at Nakatomi Plaza. Not even close. He's mostly shooting up bad guys. In this chapter, however, John learns more about his enemies, and he finds out Hans is the person in charge.

Hans. That bad, bad, very bad guy. So evil, and yet somehow so cool. Kind of like, uh, I don't know...Professor Snape?

Yes, they're played by the same actor. The fact that I chose two movies starring Alan Rickman says a lot.

Mostly it says I really like Alan Rickman, and I always will.

Always.

Sniff.

Anyway, John also needs an ally at this point, and he'll find one—in Al, an LAPD police officer with an awesomely tragic backstory of his own. Oh, and Al's wife is pregnant with their first baby, something which garners immediate sympathy for him. Now you're rooting for both John and Al. Let the (fun and) games begin.

7

FUN AND GAMES

You promised your reader fun and games, and in this chapter, you deliver.

"But wait," you say. "I never promised anyone anything."

Au contraire, mon ami. You did indeed make them a promise. You did it in your blurb and your pitch, and your tagline. You did it when you made this the part of the story your reader would look forward to most, which is why this concept is often called, "The Promise of the Premise."

Think about your favorite books and movies. The fun and games section is always the best part. It's when your detective will find the most clues, when your action hero will dodge the most bullets, and when your romantic couple truly begins to fall in love. This is also the part of your book during which your main character explores their new world, and the audience is entertained by the premise they have been promised. Think about Katniss surviving in the woods (you knew she had survival skills!) and Elle surviving at Harvard (you knew she was more intelligent than people realized!). These are the moments your reader imagined and looked forward to during the first act of your book, so it's up to you to give them what they wanted.

"The Promise of the Premise" is simple. It's the part of the book your readers have waited for in gleeful anticipation, and it's usually the reason they bought your book in the first place.

When someone reads your blurb, this is what they were excited to see. This is what they have wanted to experience since the moment they started reading.

For those reading the first book in the *Harry Potter* series, one thing they've been waiting for are the wizarding classes. When they read the back cover of the first book and learned he's secretly a wizard about to go to a magical boarding school, this is what they wanted most to see.

Harry in potions class.

Harry riding on a broom.

Harry learning how to use his wand.

It's the part of the book that brings a smile to your reader's face. The games in the FUN AND GAMES section might not be terribly fun at all, but they are still important.

Think of *The Hunger Games*. The games most definitely are not enjoyable in this story, but the reader still wants to see something, and it's very specific.

From the opening image on, the reader has known Katniss has skills. She can hide, she has knowledge about the outdoors, and she's good with an arrow. She's a survivor, and they want to see her do so.

As you may have already guessed, often this chapter is about showing how a character has a secret ability or talent. Harry is naturally gifted at riding a broom and the reader learns he will become the youngest seeker in Hogwarts' quidditch history. It's exciting when the main character begins to blossom and shine, and it happens in *The Hunger Games,* too.

Remember the thrill you got when Katniss first demonstrated her archery skills to the other tributes? It's like you had an inside look, and your reader will feel the same way in this chapter of your book. They know your main character is worthy and has secret talents, and it's fun for everyone when the rest of the characters in the book finally figure it out.

This applies to *Legally Blonde,* too. As Elle is prancing around Harvard in her Prada's, we're catching glimpses of her intelligence and out-of-the-box thinking. Although cowed at first by her professors and classmates, she's beginning to show she isn't what she seems. She's got a lawyer's brain hidden under all those beautiful highlights.

And although the fun and games section of *Die Hard* isn't exactly fun, we're learning a lot more about John. He is not your average, run-of-the-mill police officer. This man seems more like someone with special ops training. He has an arsenal of impressive skills, which is why he's able to survive and take out the bad guys one by one.

Remember the "ho, ho, ho" written in blood on the body of Karl's brother, Tony? Not exactly fun, but John must have thought it was funny. He also thought it was an excellent way to get into the terrorists' heads because he knows angry people make poor choices. John, like Elle, is a lot smarter than we first realized.

Oh, and a *Die Hard* related side note: In case you didn't know, the famous Russian ballet dancer, Alexander Godunov, played Karl. He was more than good enough (get it??) for the role. In fact, he was perfect, in all his big, blond,

Russian, sexy dancer glory. He was worthy—and that is what your character must prove next.

Are they worthy?

Are they up to the challenge?

Can they really do this?

Gosh, I hope so. I guess we'll find out.

8

PROVING THEY ARE WORTHY

After breaking into Act II, there will be several chapters where the protagonist learns about their new world. They might be practicing magic, discovering how to survive a dystopian battle to the death, learning how to get through law school, or figuring out how to mess with Hans. Chapters Six and Seven are full of this stuff, and there needs to be conflict and tension and exciting twist and turns. This builds and builds until (boom!) the first battle, which is also the first pinch point.

Remember Nessie the Plot Monster?

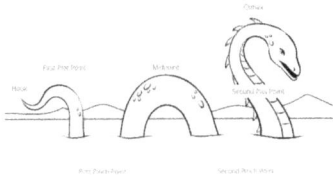

As we already discussed, you know you have to have plot points (the incidents which will directly impact what will happen next in the story and change the story's direction). And you must also have pinch points (when the character is under pressure and must react to a plot point).

That is what's going on now, in this first fight with the forces of evil. But let me be straight here—this doesn't have to be an actual fight, and the forces might not be completely evil. It is, however, the first significant interaction your character has with the antagonist.

This is a big moment, so you should make the situation as dire as possible. Often, when someone gives you writing advice, they say it's wise to think of the worst thing that can happen to your character and then make something even worse happen. Insult upon injury. Salt poured into an open wound. Lemon juice in a paper cut.

You get the idea, and this is where you want to do it, so grab your saltshaker (or your lemon) and get ready. You need to ask, "What's the worst thing that could happen to my main character?" And then ask yourself (with a wicked gleam in your eyes), "How can I make them suffer even more?"

And you'll know how to do it because you're evil. Brilliant, but evil.

In *Harry Potter*, there are a few battles being fought at around the same time. First comes the sorting hat, when Harry begs not to be put into Slytherin. He wins the battle when he gets into Gryffindor.

As you can probably understand, it's not always a beat-them-up, physical sort of battle. Often, it's low key. Sometimes it's internal.

But a significant real pinch point in *Harry Potter* is when Harry and Draco fight on brooms over Neville's

Rememberall. Do you recall the moment that happened? How exciting it was to know Harry could handle a broom like a boss? But it was also nerve-wracking because you knew the whole time it was dangerous, forbidden behavior. Madam Hooch, the flight instructor, told the students specifically *not* to fly while she was gone, and yet Harry jumped onto his broom like he'd been riding it every day of his life.

Harry proves his worth when he battles Draco. He may have sucked at potions class, but he rocks broom riding. And that is important.

Katniss proves herself worthy when she shows her archery skills during a private training session. Unfortunately, the gamemakers are way too focused on their meal, and they miss it. This ticks Katniss off, and she responds as any good archer would—by using her bow to shoot an apple in the mouth of a roasted pig on the buffet table. That gets the attention of the gamemakers (and everyone else), and she earns a training score of eleven, which is the highest of any tribute.

Katniss is playing along with the image and the role they want her to play, and she's getting oddly good at it. And the fact that food is involved in this scene, when most of her district is living on the verge of starvation, is very symbolic and important.

In *Legally Blonde*, Vivian tricks poor Elle into showing up at a party dressed as a Playboy bunny. Elle's battle isn't only with the snarky Vivian, though—it's also with Warner. We feel Elle's pain and humiliation as she walks into the party. But does she let it defeat her? Heck, no. She lifts her chin, wears the bunny ears and cottontail proudly, and, after leaving the party, she marches straight to the bookstore to purchase a laptop. Her battle might seem small in compar-

---

ison to Katniss's, but it's significant to her. And buying the laptop is nothing less than a declaration of war.

For John, it is, of course, an actual battle, but it's not only one fight. He's taking out the terrorists one by one and proving he's worthy. Proving he has the skills to defeat these guys, even if it seems hopeless. Even if he doesn't appear to be winning at all. Because that's the most important thing about the first pinch point. Your character doesn't usually win the first battle, but they live to fight another day.

Another essential element of this chapter is the antagonist. They rear their ugly head and make it known that they want something the main character has. In *Legally Blonde*, you can see it in how Vivian is so jealous of Elle. But the true antagonists in this movie are all the people who discounted Elle—people like Warner and Professor Callaghan, not Vivian. Even though Vivian caused the first battle, she did it only because she wants to secure her position as Warner's fiancée, and her hatred of Elle comes from her own insecurities and doubt.

On the other hand, the antagonist might have a score to settle or want the main character to do something. That is true in *Die Hard*. The more John succeeds, the more it becomes a personal issue for Hans.

At this point in the story, the main character most likely has no idea what's happening (YET), but they still find themselves at the center of the conflict. The stakes should always seem like life and death to the protagonist.

In the case of Elle Woods, you can see the death of her dreams of fitting in at Harvard and getting her beau back. That is shown poignantly when Warner tells her she isn't smart enough to get the prestigious internship with Professor Callaghan. You see true understanding dawning in her eyes as she says, "I'll never be good enough for you, will I?"

As demonstrated by Elle, this first battle is when a complete change occurs. It's the "death" of the character's former self. If your protagonist doesn't have their self-identity shaken to its roots during the first battle, you need to make this scene bigger. This is a significant turning point in your story. Your character is being pinched and feeling the pressure, but even if they don't completely succeed, they prove they are up to the challenge.

9

THE STAKES ARE RAISED

In this chapter, things get serious—mega serious. There has to be a point when the antagonist is revealed or at least hinted at. Many times, this is a red herring sort of chapter when your character might think they know who the antagonist is, but they don't. They are getting closer though, and with each move they make, the sense of danger increases.

There are no plot points or pinch points here. You're simply making things more and more exciting as you approach the midpoint of your novel. You want to keep your reader guessing, which is why the red herrings are so helpful. And you want to keep it as interesting as possible so your reader will continue turning the pages. This can be a saggy part of your book, so don't neglect it. Make it count.

In *Harry Potter*, Harry and his friends find the three-headed dog Fluffy when they go up to the forbidden third floor. The stakes are raised both because Fluffy is obviously dangerous, and because Hermione sees a trap door beneath Fluffy and realizes the dog is guarding something. They think it's somehow connected to Professor Snape, and they're pretty convinced he's the bad guy (red herring!), but they are going to get a huge surprise.

There aren't really any red herrings in *The Hunger Games*. We know the gamemakers are bad. We know the Capitol is bad. We know President Snow is bad. And we know the career tributes are bad. The tricky part is Peeta. Is he as good as he pretends to be, and does he have Katniss's best interest at heart? She isn't sure, but she goes along with his unexpected plan and fakes a romantic connection with him to score points with viewers. But it's a double-edged sword. As Katniss becomes more popular, she's more of a threat to the other tributes. And when Peeta opens up to her and tells her he wants to die on his own terms, it strikes a chord in Katniss, too.

In *Legally Blonde*, we watch the memorable scene when Elle shuts Warner down in Professor Callaghan's class, and the professor asks if she plans to apply for his internship. She is taken aback, and honored by his suggestion, but we're fooled. It seems like Professor Callaghan is a good guy.

Spoiler alert: He isn't.

Back at Nakatomi Plaza, John is on the roof calling for help, and he's frantic. He has no doubt Hans is a bad guy, but now he is figuring out Hans is probably psychotic. Hans isn't doing this to make a political statement or to free random comrades in prison. His motives are purely financial, which makes him a special kind of evil. When this becomes clear, John understands the hostages might be expendable in Hans's mind, and he knows he's going to have to kill a lot of bad guys.

The stakes have been raised, and now innocent people

might die. What will John do? He's in a tough spot. It's time for him to face the truth, and it's also time for something else that is very important.

An ultimatum.

Uh-oh.

10

TRUTH AND ULTIMATUM

Congratulations. You've reached the midpoint. You're halfway done—hooray! Give yourself a nice pat on the back, then get back to work because you still have a lot to accomplish.

In Chapter Ten, your character moves from reaction to action. They know they must proactively do something to stop the antagonist, so they go from being a victim to becoming a warrior.

This is a big change. HUGE. After the first battle (the first pinch point), your character continues to face new challenges, but they're still stuck in a defensive role. They might be making plans and coming up with ways to defeat the antagonist or reach their goal, but mostly they're waiting around for something to happen and reacting to events or circumstances beyond their control.

This is tough, especially because it seems like if they try to solve any issue at all, they end up being thwarted or making things worse instead of better. They might accidentally hurt someone they care about or lose the trust and respect of their family and friends.

It's likely they have secrets now. Big secrets. They start questioning their identity and worldview, which leads to what can be seen as a personality crisis, and which also leads to a shift in perspective.

All these things happen up to halfway through the novel, and the midpoint marks the place where the protagonist decides to take action. They stop just being a victim and reacting to events and vow to do whatever it takes to win.

They'll probably form a new goal at this time, and even if they aren't sure how to achieve it (yet), they'll feel a deep conviction toward it. That conviction might be based on anger, or a desire for revenge, or a new perspective, or increased self-confidence—it doesn't matter. The conviction itself is what matters.

The midpoint is also the moment in your novel when everything is super great, or everything is really awful. There is often a party at this point or a gathering. In *Harry Potter*, it's the Halloween party (things are great!), followed by Harry and Ron finding out Hermione is crying in a bathroom close to where a dangerous troll has been spotted. Hermione has no idea, and she's in terrible danger (things are awful!).

This is an important chapter for the antagonist. The reader might not know who the bad guy is yet, but the antagonist should be the one calling all the shots at this point. The bad guy is after something, and that something is tied to the protagonist. The villain is totally in control, but this is the turning point. This is when things change.

At this point in the book, Harry notices a wound on Snape's leg. He and his friends had already begun to suspect Snape is the bad guy, and those fears are increased when Ron and Hermione see Snape muttering something during Harry's first quidditch match. They think Snape is jinxing Harry's broom, and their suspicions appear to be justified, but things are still unclear. They know they are missing something, and they're poking around in the dark trying to figure it out.

This chapter is also a time of false highs and false lows. For example, Harry and Ron took action and fought the troll after the Halloween Party in the Great Hall. That is a false high because they got in trouble for it, even if they each received five points for Gryffindor for "sheer, dumb luck."

In *The Hunger Games,* Katniss goes up the tube and enters the games. Whether it's a false high or low depends on the reader's expectations. If they thought Katniss would come out of the tube like a cute, teenage version of Rambo, it's a false low. She isn't Rambo. But if they think she's going to be in trouble as soon as she exits (remember how nervous she was as she waited?), it's a false high. Things are only okay because she doesn't engage. She listens to the advice she received and runs away like a little bunny and hides. Katniss is not a coward. She's a smart girl, and she's also a survivor.

Just a note: The visual of her rising on that platform as she enters the unknown area is incredible. It's symbolic of the rising stakes in the story, and perfectly done.

The midpoint of *Legally Blonde* is also a party—the horrible not-a-costume-party in Chapter Eight. We all remember how Elle in her bunny costume was humiliated by Vivian and insulted by Warner, and how she decided to prove herself to both of them by getting a laptop (obviously a great solution). But the aftereffects of what happened at the party are seen here, at the midpoint.

Elle begins wearing a new hat (a cute, crocheted

number). The hat keeps her warm, makes her look like the others, and covers her golden locks. She starts studying more (aka carrying big, heavy law books around), and doing better at school. She is determined, and she gets the coveted internship, but that is a false high. Elle's goal is still to prove herself to Warner and to others, not to become a better lawyer or grow as a person.

In *Die Hard* there is no party, and there definitely aren't any crocheted hats. John is on the offensive and killing more bad guys. But now, because he has an ally in Al, things are going in a better direction. Also, John has the detonators Hans needs to complete the job. The situation is looking up, but that is a false high, because the police try to move in, and mistakes start happening. They play into the terrorists' hands, and John can't stop them.

Or can he?

Maybe John needs to re-evaluate. And that is exactly what happens in good old Chapter Eleven.

11

THE MAN IN THE MIRROR MOMENT

I should refer to this as the "person" in the mirror moment, but since I hear the Michael Jackson song in my head every time I think about this chapter, I'm sticking with it. The point of titling each chapter is not to sound clever or insightful. I'm trying to help you remember what it's about as clearly as possible.

I set high goals. The less complicated something is, the better.

But this chapter is exactly what it sounds like. It's when the character looks at themselves and their goals and understands their goals have changed.

I love this chapter. I think it's important, but until I took a closer look at how things are plotted, I often skipped it in my own books. What a huge mistake! This is an incredible opportunity for your character to take a good hard look at themselves and reassess their goals and desires.

In *Harry Potter*, there is an actual mirror, the Mirror of Erised. When Harry looks into it, it shows him everything he thought he wanted: his parents and a happy familial unit. His parents are dead, of course, and deep inside him is a huge wound. The mirror offers him comfort, but soon he becomes addicted to its lure.

Dumbledore steps in and helps by explaining what Harry sees in the mirror isn't real. He also tells Harry the mirror is dangerous because it shows the deepest and darkest desires of a person's heart. Because of that, and out of concern for Harry, Dumbledore tells him he's moving the mirror and Harry shouldn't try to find it for the sake of his own mental health.

Katniss grapples with the fact that if she wants to survive, she'll have to play by the rules of the game, which she despises. When she looks into the (figurative) mirror, she might not like what she sees, or who she is becoming. She wants to defy the gamemakers and keep her humanity, but can she?

Elle begins to appreciate the power she'll have as a lawyer when she helps the hairdresser get back her dog. Being a successful lawyer is important to her now. Not to prove something to Warner, but because she wants to prove to herself she can do it.

In *Die Hard*, John's moment comes after the slimeball character Ellis foolishly steps in and attempts to negotiate with the terrorists. It's a fatal mistake. John tries to stop him but can't, and Ellis ends up dead. John talks to Al, devastated by the decision he had to make. As John realizes with even better clarity that his family is everything, we understand he's not the same person he was at the beginning of the story.

The Man in the Mirror. Are you asking if he's changed his ways?

If so, the answer should be a resounding, "Yes."

12

_____

MAKING A PLAN

Your character has gone from victim to warrior. They've had their person-in-the-mirror moment and have different goals now. They are in it to win it. They understand that they have a critical role to play, something only they can do, and they realize they've been trusted with an important task.

This is also when we have the second confrontation with the antagonist.

Remember Nessie the Plot Monster?

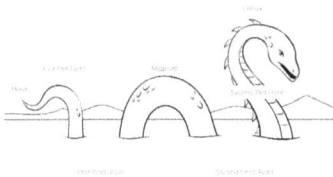

The midpoint was a plot point (something that changed

the direction of the plot). This chapter is the second pinch point: A reaction to the midpoint.

It's all up and down, up and down, but when it comes to the actual battle in this section of the book, it might not be with the antagonist directly. It could be with one of the antagonist's partners in crime, or even with one of their minions. No matter who it is, they cause major problems for our protagonist.

So, what about this is different from the first pinch point? Well, it seems like this usually plays out in one of two ways. Either the antagonist (and/or their compadres) goes after our poor protagonist directly, or our protagonist takes some sort of action that results in a confrontation.

What can it be?

Maybe they set a trap for the bad guy. Maybe the bad guy sets a trap for them. Maybe someone the protagonist cares about is hurt or killed or taken prisoner or disappears. If this happens, it makes our protagonist feel personally responsible—and even more determined. Our hero has suddenly realized things are much worse than they anticipated, and they may have underestimated the antagonist. They've also become aware the chances of success are slim, but even that knowledge does not stop them from trying.

In *Harry Potter*, Harry and Ron are instructed by Hermione to sneak into the restricted section of the library over winter break. Harry is gifted an invisibility cloak for Christmas, so he's able to get in, but is nearly caught by Filch. He escapes, and that's when he first finds the Mirror of Erised.

You can see this isn't exactly in chronological order, but it still fits. When Hermione returns to school after their break is over, she finds the information she's been searching for, and recognizes Fluffy must be guarding the sorcerer's stone. The three of them sneak out to question Hagrid about it, and (once again) they end up in trouble. Draco follows them and tells on them for leaving the school after hours, but that means Draco disobeyed the rules too. Because of this, Harry, Ron, Hermione, and Draco all end up in detention...with Hagrid...in the Forbidden Forest.

What could possibly go wrong?

During the midpoint, Harry and Ron save Hermione from the troll, become more convinced Snape is behind everything, learn some hard truths from the Mirror of Erised, and figure out what Fluffy is guarding. But their actions have consequences, and now, as part of their punishment, they must help Hagrid hunt for an injured unicorn.

This is an important part of the story, and a pinch point. Why?

Because when Harry finds the body of the unicorn, and sees who is drinking the unicorn's blood, he grasps (with the help of Firenze the centaur), exactly who and what he is up against—Lord Voldemort himself.

Harry has taken action. He did so when he went after the troll, when he found Fluffy, and when he sought out Hagrid to confirm his suspicions. He's in warrior mode now, acting instead of reacting, but these actions have consequences. The consequences this time are detention in the forest and an encounter with the dark lord himself.

In *The Hunger Games,* Katniss is stuck up in a tree. Literally. And a bunch of career tributes are waiting below to kill her as soon as she comes down. Peeta is with them, which complicates things for her. But Rue helps her by pointing out the tracker jacker nest. Katniss realizes it's a kill or be killed situation, so she saws off the nest and drops it on the other tributes, killing one of them. She took action. She's become a warrior. She made a plan. But now she also faces consequences, because (uh-oh) she's been stung by the tracker jackers, too.

In *Legally Blonde,* Elle now looks and acts more like a lawyer, and it turns out she knows the person she'll help defend during Professor Callaghan's internship. Her name is Brooke. She's a Kappa Nu, like Elle, who has been falsely accused of killing her husband. While the other lawyers doubt Brooke's innocence, Elle believes in her, and is determined to help. She takes action and visits Brooke in jail. Brooke explains her alibi (she was having liposuction on her bottom) but begs Elle not to tell anyone. Elle promises to keep her secret, and Elle is a woman of her word. Even though the others try to push her into spilling the beans, she won't, but she still contributes. She takes initiative when she hears they need someone to interview the ex-wife of the murdered man at a spa. One of the other lawyers sarcastically asks, "Isn't the spa your home planet?" but Elle refuses to be baited. She makes a plan and heads to the spa.

In *Die Hard,* John meets Hans, the antagonist, face to face. Hans tries to trick John into thinking he's a hostage who escaped, and we're wondering—has John been fooled? Is this going to be the end for our brave hero? John even gives Hans a gun. Yikes.

But—yippy-ky-yay—it turns out this is not John's first rodeo. When Hans tries to shoot him, we realize the gun has no bullets in it (clever John!), but in the scuffle that ensues, John loses something important. The detonators. Now, once again, Hans has the power.

Uh-oh. We're screwed. Which is what Chapter Thirteen is all about.

13

OOPS, WE'RE SCREWED

The bad guys are succeeding and closing in on our brave hero. The plan our protagonist made in the previous chapter has now gone horribly wrong. Their mistake may have been caused by bad intel or maybe their assumptions were incorrect. Either way, there will be consequences. The antagonist has been given a chance to regroup.

Right now, the main character feels a plethora of emotions, including doubt in their own ability to make things right, and fear that there will be even more consequences for their actions.

This is a chapter of escalating tensions and rising stakes. It's leading up to the second (and final) plot point. You'll recall that every chapter before a plot point is full of rising action. This one is no different.

Remember Nessie the Plot Monster?

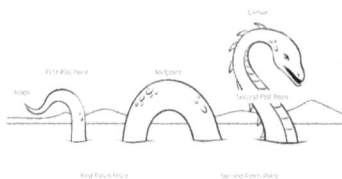

This is the final climb. Right up the beast's neck.

In *Harry Potter,* things are getting darker and scarier. Harry knows Voldemort is back in the picture, but Harry and his friends are still convinced Snape is somehow involved. They think Snape is working for Voldemort and trying to get the sorcerer's stone for him, and it feels like there is nothing anyone can do to stop it.

Harry is in great danger, but one thought comforts Harry and his friends. They know as long as Dumbledore is around, he will keep Harry safe. It's their sole consolation, and they are counting on it. Big time.

In *The Hunger Games,* Katniss is a mess. Although she succeeded in scaring away the other tributes (and killing one) with the tracker jackers, she was stung, too. She's vulnerable. She's hallucinating. She is in some serious trouble. But she manages to get a bow and arrows from the fallen tribute, and she has two unexpected allies. Peeta saves her first by telling her to run, and Rue saves her by caring for her and helping Katniss recover from the tracker jacker stings. They pair up and a friendship forms. Rue reminds Katniss of her sister, and they decide to fight the bad guys together.

In *Legally Blonde,* things are bad, too. Callaghan calls Elle to his office, and hits on her. It's a devastating moment for Elle. She's repulsed, but she also doubts her own self-worth. She thought she earned her spot on Callaghan's team, but did she? She isn't certain, and it feels like, once again, someone thinks she's nothing more than a pretty face.

And in *Die Hard,* John gets away from Hans, but now things are bad. Clever Hans shot up the glass windows, so John had to run over broken glass in his bare feet. He also had to leave the detonators behind, which puts everyone in even greater danger.

In this chapter, we get a bonus, because John has another man in the mirror moment. This time, he's in a bathroom with a literal mirror—like Harry. Unlike Mr. Potter, however, John is hurt. He's exhausted and bloody and picking pieces of glass out of his poor bare feet. Things are not looking good. John is in big trouble and the FBI is making things worse. They are playing right into Hans's plans.

Oh, no. Chapter Fourteen is coming, and guess what?

It's only going to get worse. We are super screwed now.

14

UH-OH. WE ARE SUPER SCREWED

Here we are. The second plot point. The moment our heroic main character realizes they've lost every inch they'd gained, or they've come to understand what they now have has no meaning to them at all. Their goal looks even more impossible and unattainable than ever before.

Oh, and this is usually when someone (or something) dies.

You have to make sure your character is really suffering now. Their pain can be either physical or emotional, but it's the death of something old (like a belief or a goal or a plan) that makes way for something new and better to be born.

Hopefully.

You'll remember that a plot point is a significant incident that directly impacts what will happen next in the story and changes the story's direction. This is our last one, so it has to be a doozy.

The second plot point in *Harry Potter* arises after Harry finally comes to terms with the fact that Voldemort wants to steal the stone. He still thinks Snape is involved, but now he acknowledges Voldemort is the one pulling the strings. Yes,

Harry saw Voldemort drinking the unicorn blood, which was a shock (and super nasty) (poor unicorn), but it's in this chapter that something significant happens to change the direction of the story.

Harry learns Hagrid, while drunk and gambling (in typical Hagrid fashion), may have accidentally told a stranger the secret of how to get Fluffy (the three-headed dog), to fall asleep.

Uh-oh.

Now Harry has no choice. He must take action. If he doesn't, and if Voldemort succeeds, Harry and everyone he cares about will die, and everything that has meaning to him now will be destroyed.

Heavy baggage for an eleven-year-old.

Things are disintegrating quickly in *The Hunger Games,* too. Katniss has grown close to Rue and taken on the role of older sister and protector. But, because of a plan Katniss made, Rue gets stuck in a trap. As Katniss frees her, another tribute appears and throws a spear. Katniss responds instinctively—by killing the other tribute with an arrow. It's the first time Katniss has killed anyone on purpose, but it's too late. As Katniss turns to check on Rue, she realizes the spear, the one intended for her, has hit Rue instead, and it's a fatal wound.

In *Legally Blonde,* Elle faces a dark moment, too. Callaghan hit on her. She's in shock. And although she and Vivian had formed a tentative friendship, Vivian sees Callaghan sexually harassing Elle and misinterprets the situation. She thinks Elle is in a consensual relationship, and Elle is sleeping her way to the top. Vivian had begun to admire Elle, especially when she refused to spill the beans about Brooke's alibi, but now? Vivian seems to feel a sense of betrayal, which is why she lashes out at Elle with her accusations. And it's more than Elle can take. It's one more person who doesn't take her seriously, and she doubts anyone ever will.

And in *Die Hard,* John is also having a rough time. The Feds shut off the power, the terrorists got into the vault, and we know, somehow, things are going to get much, much worse.

John knows it, too. And he gets so upset, he partially blows up Nakatomi Plaza.

Oops. Things are getting dark now.

15

DARK NIGHT OF THE SOUL

Different plotting gurus use different terms to describe this moment in the story. "The Dark Night of the Soul" is one of them. I don't know who came up with it first, but it was used as the name of a poem written by a Spanish mystic in the 16th century, so maybe I should give him credit.

Thank you, St. John of the Cross, you awesome mystic poet you!

You may not know much about St. John, or Spanish mystics in general, but you will understand this moment in your story. It's when your main character hits rock bottom. They are wallowing in self-pity and feeling hopeless. It's the good old reliable "Why hast thou forsaken me, Lord?" moment.

They are mourning the loss of someone or something. It might be the death of an actual person, or just the death of their dream, but they feel it. They reach the lowest of all the low points in the story.

It can happen in different ways. Maybe the hero's super fantastic plan failed. Maybe they lost someone close to them. Whatever it is, the worst has happened, and right now it feels like the antagonist has won. This is the second pinch point, and no matter how hard the hero tried to fix it, things have spiraled right out of control.

It's a moment of intense despair and devastating loss. Everything our protagonist feared could happen, has happened.

They are destroyed.

They cannot win.

They give up.

There's no hope and they feel like a big, fat, guilty failure.

Why?

Because whatever happened is a result of their actions or a flaw in their character. That's heavy—and depressing. But what happens when you fall? You pick yourself right back up and keep trying.

Things have changed, though. This loss has made your main character appreciate that whatever they've been holding on to (which is often nothing more than a desire for things to go back to normal) is gone. There is no chance to attain that goal, and the only way to move forward is to change and go in a new direction.

Due to this experience, they comprehend they are willing to sacrifice anything, even their own dreams, for the good of others. And this is when they finally become the hero they were always meant to be.

In *Harry Potter,* Harry and his friends go to Dumbledore (the only person who can keep Harry safe) for help but learn from McGonagall that Dumbledore is gone. That is bad news indeed. It's a bleak moment, but it's also the moment the kids understand it is truly up to them to fix this.

In *The Hunger Games,* the low moment for Katniss is

incredibly poignant and sad. If you don't weep during this scene, you have no heart. It's the darkest of all dark nights of the soul, because poor, sweet, spunky Rue is dying. Katniss sings to her as she passes away, but the death of Rue is also the death of everything Katniss once held dear.

The death of the friend who'd become like a sister to her.

The death of her faith in others.

Katniss is gutted, and so is everyone who reads this scene or sees it played out in the movie. It's perfect in its portrayal of utter despair, and it leaves us wondering—how can Katniss possibly get over this?

Elle is also suffering. She feels like she's a failure.

She failed her friend, Brooke, who may go to jail without Elle's help.

She failed as a lawyer.

Her dream of proving herself worthy is gone. She quits the case. She's done. She tried to become someone serious and failed, so now it's all over. Elle is giving up.

In *Die Hard,* John is having a dark moment, too. He's hurt and bleeding. He feels unappreciated and hopeless. He asks Al to find his wife, Holly, if things end poorly and tell her all the things he couldn't say. He truly doesn't think he'll see his family again.

To make matters worse, John figures out the roof is rigged to explode. Hans is planning to kill all the hostages, including Holly.

And, unbeknownst to John, this is also the part of the story when a reporter goes to Holly's house and interviews John and Holly's children. Upon seeing the interview, Hans puts two and two together. He finds the photo of John and Holly and realizes he has the perfect hostage now. Holly is in even greater danger; she's become a target, and it's all John's fault.

Rock bottom. It looks different for different characters, but it has to be the lowest of the low. And how are you going to get your hero out of this slump?

Well, that is what Chapter Sixteen is all about.

16

PEP TALK

When the poor protagonist thinks there is no way they can possibly survive, someone steps in and gives them just the pep talk they needed. It might be a friend. It might be a lover. It might be a whole group of people. It doesn't matter. The pep talk is what gives them the push they need. It's what propels them from rock bottom and makes them dust themselves off and get back into the fight.

In *Harry Potter,* the kids sneak into the trap door Fluffy was guarding and face many different obstacles. It culminates when Ron sacrifices himself during a wizard chess match. He does it at great personal risk because wizard chess is not for the faint of heart, but it has to be done. This is when the pep talk occurs. Ron and Hermione both tell Harry he is the one who must go on, because he's the only one who stands a chance at being victorious. It's his battle, and they all know it, but it's Ron and Hermione who believe Harry will win.

In *The Hunger Games,* it's Rue who gives Katniss a pep talk. Right before she dies, she makes Katniss promise that she will win for both of them and asks Katniss to sing her a song. Katniss does, and then, in an act of rebellion against the Capitol, she surrounds Rue's body with flowers. She honors Rue with a sort of funeral, reminding everyone Rue was a person. A child. And this idea, this thoughtfulness, this humanity, is the opposite of what viewers have come to expect from the games.

When Katniss finishes, she rises to her feet, touches her fingers to her lips, and raises her arm—using a traditional District 12 salute to honor Rue. It's one of the best moments in the film, and her simple gesture lights a spark. Although Katniss doesn't know it, her salute and her defiance set off riots in Rue's district and beyond, and the people in charge are not happy about it at all.

Previously, Peeta had said he wanted to die on his own terms, in a way that would show the Capitol he was more than just a pawn. His words were, perhaps, part of what inspired Katniss to give Rue that funeral, in direct defiance to everything the games symbolize. Later (in the book, not the movie), a gift comes to Katniss. It's a loaf of bread, and she understands the significance. It's from District 11, and it's a thank you for what she did for Rue. That is a sort of pep talk as well. Knowing she has the support and gratitude from another district inspires her.

The whole scene is so powerful. From Rue's final words, to her death, to Katniss's grief, and finally to her resolve. Can you think of it without getting chills? I can't. It's beautifully done. And that's what makes it so powerful.

Elle's pep talk comes from Emmett, the hunky lawyer guy. He encourages her not to quit the case, and so does her client, Brooke. And when Vivian realizes she didn't see what she thought she saw, and that Professor Callaghan was harassing Elle, I imagine she gives Elle a pep talk, too. It's not shown in the film, but I wish it had been, because I think Vivian's words were probably important, and perhaps instrumental in getting Elle to step back into the fight. But the most important pep talk of all comes from Professor Stromwell.

At the beginning of the movie, Professor Stromwell calls Elle out on the first day of class for not being prepared. But at Elle's moment of crisis and intense self-doubt, it's Professor Stromwell who encourages Elle not to give up. And knowing Professor Stromwell believes in her changes everything.

In *Die Hard*, once again, Al encourages John. These two remind me of a couple that meets online and gets close on a deep and profound level before ever meeting in person. They know each other, and they understand each other. Al has shared his secret pain (the fact that he accidentally killed an unarmed kid and now can't shoot a gun), and John shares his as well. John, in many ways, failed as a husband. He sees it now and understands his mistakes. But does the knowledge come too late? Al doesn't think so, and that's part of what keeps John in the game.

The pep talk. It's a simple concept, but it's so important. I won't go into greater detail because I think the examples speak for themselves. The important thing to know is that the pep talk is exactly what your character needs to hear at precisely the right time. And it's up to you, as a writer, to make it happen, because that is what causes your character to break into Act III. The final act. Huzzah!

17

IT'S ON

Act III. Your story is on the verge of reaching its exciting conclusion.

Thanks to the wonderful pep talk from our B story character, our hero is ready and willing to fight another day. They break into Act III directly because of what happened in the previous chapter. Included in that pep talk was some nugget of truth about our main character.

What were those truths?

Harry was the only one who could move on in the wizard chess match because Harry is the only one who can defeat the villain.

Katniss is inspired not only to survive; thanks to Rue's pep talk, she is now determined to win. She's also mad, and her anger is directed toward the true villains in this story— President Snow and the Capitol.

Elle is determined as well. With the support of her new love interest (Emmett), her former archnemesis (Vivian), someone she admires (Professor Stromwell), and the one person who believed in her all along (Brooke), Elle puts on her big girl heels and walks back into the courtroom.

And with Al's encouragement, John gets his second wind—and the emotional boost he needs to complete his task.

The pep talks were important, because they made your character stand up, dust off, gird their loins, and ride into Act III. The final battle. The do or die moment. The last chance the character has to fix things. And they have to go big to defeat the pesky antagonist, because there is no going home.

In *Harry Potter,* the pep talk from Ron and Hermione gave Harry the courage to go to the scary cave, where someone (or something) is waiting for him. But it is not at all what he expects, and Harry gets a big surprise.

Some unexpected things happen in *The Hunger Games,* too. As a result of the reaction in several of the districts over Rue's death and Katniss's humanizing moment, the gamemakers alter the rules. Now *two* tributes can win if they're from the same district. That changes everything, and Katniss takes an active step to find Peeta. She saves him, and now everyone is inspired by what they think is a love story. Katniss plays into it because she wants to survive, but we aren't sure how much is real and how much is theater.

In *Legally Blonde,* Elle accepts the challenge to represent Brooke, and Professor Callaghan is fired from the case. Now it's up to Elle to save her friend and prove herself worthy.

And in *Die Hard,* John figures out the hostages are on the roof, and it's going to blow up. He rushes up to save them, but the FBI guys (who are jerky jerk faces) think John is trying to kill the hostages. They shoot at him, even though John is a total hero.

John barely survives. He is forced to grab a rope and

swing down to one of the lower floors and crash in through a window (not an easy task!). He makes it to safety, but he can't save the FBI guys. They end up getting blown to bits.

Do we feel bad for them?

No.

Do we feel bad for John?

Yes, and now we're also afraid for him.

John saved the hostages, which is great, but there is still more work left to do. It's not going to be easy for our brave hero. Because you know what's going to happen next, right?

Things are going to get worse.

Oh, no.

Buckle up, buttercup. It's going to be a rough ride.

18
_____

PLOT TWIST

This chapter is the final kick in the cojones for our character. They are so close and inspired by their pep talk, but things do not go at all as planned. They try. They fail. The bad guy wins. Game over.

Naming this chapter was tricky. It could have been called "ULTIMATE DEFEAT" or "YOU'RE A LOSING LOSER," but "PLOT TWIST" fits because this chapter is all about fooling your reader.

Something surprising must happen, and it's not a good surprise. You cannot make things easy on your reader, right? We all know that. Think of this as one last chance to make your reader squirm. To make them worry. To make them wonder, "How the heck is the hero going to survive these insurmountable odds?"

This is the time for you, dear writer, to rub your hands together and laugh maniacally. You are the only one who knows what will happen in the end, and it's up to you to draw out the tension a little longer.

In *Harry Potter,* Harry thinks he's going to find Snape in the cave, but it's not Snape at all.

In the creepiest of all the creepy scenes in this movie, Harry finds the stammering, stuttering Professor Quirrell in the cave. Quirrell has the Mirror of Erised and is somehow speaking to Lord Voldemort. The dark lord instructs him to make Harry use the mirror, and to tell him what Harry sees. Although previously Harry had only seen his parents, now he sees himself in the mirror, holding the sorcerer's stone. Suddenly, the stone appears in Harry's pocket, and when Quirrell unwinds his turban (plot twist!), we see Lord Voldemort himself on the back of Professor Quirrell's head.

Eek!

Voldemort offers Harry everything—eternal life and the chance to get his parents back. How can Harry resist? How can this little kid stand up to the most powerful dark wizard of all time—especially when he promises exactly what Harry has always wanted?

But Harry is strong, and when he refuses, Voldemort tells Quirrell to kill Harry.

Ultimate defeat. Game over. Harry is going to die.

In *The Hunger Games,* Katniss and Peeta are doing well. Every other tribute dies except them. They are the victors! Hooray! But something is wrong (plot twist). The game isn't over yet. In a surprise move, the rules change once again, and they are faced with a terrible choice. Only one of them can win.

What are they going to do? We know Peeta loves Katniss, and Katniss maybe sort of has feelings for Peeta, too. They can't kill each other...can they?

For a moment, we're left wondering, but then (second plot twist), Katniss pulls out a handful of poisonous night-lock berries. They decide to commit suicide live on television. They'd rather both die than kill each other, and it's the ultimate act of defiance. They choose their own outcome, thumbing their noses at the gamemakers for one last and final time, but it's another ultimate defeat. After fighting so hard to survive, they are now going to die in a way that's totally unexpected—by taking their own lives.

In the court room, things are getting tense. Elle has already proven the pool boy lied when he said he'd been having an affair with Brooke. Elle has been so confident, but now we see her struggling. People are laughing at her. And we begin to wonder, is she out of her depth? Emmett, Brooke, and Vivian are still nodding encouragingly, but can Elle pull it off?

As the victim's daughter sits on the stand, saying she saw Brooke commit the crime, Elle flounders. Plot twist! We didn't expect her to fail, but she asks the same questions over and over again, and we have no idea where she is going with them.

How can Elle possibly succeed? It's another ultimate defeat moment.

In *Die Hard,* John may have saved everyone else, but Hans has Holly. John knows he has only two bullets left, but he will not give up. He cannot let Holly die. We expect him to fight, but instead (plot twist) he puts down his weapon and raises his hands in defeat.

Ultimate defeat.

Game over.

Or is it?

19

SURPRISE WIN

We've reached the climactic scene. The top of the mountain on your rising action chart. The grand finale. The highest point on Nessie the Plot Monster's head. This is when your hero somehow, against all odds, defeats the antagonist and pulls out an unexpected victory.

But how?

By using the theme, of course! The nugget of truth they heard about in the first chapter now makes sense to them at last. They finally get it, thanks to the experience gained from the A Story and context garnered from the B Story. Act III is about everything coming together, and this is when it happens. In one powerful swoop.

When Harry (the boy who lived) fights back, his touch kills Quirrell, and Voldemort disappears in a scary puff of black smoke.

At the last possible second, both Katniss (the survivor) and Peeta are allowed to win.

Because Elle (who is smarter than she seems) knows the rules of hair perming, she proves the daughter is lying and saves her client.

John (that stubborn, stubborn man) refuses to give up once again. He pulls a gun out from behind his back and saves Holly.

Or does he?

We worry a bit because this is an action movie. Things never end as you think they'll end, right? So, although it looks like John has defeated the villain and saved the damsel in distress, Hans grabs Holly by the wrist as he flies out the window and pulls her along with him.

Uh-oh. We didn't expect that to happen. But at this point, we know John is going to save the day once again, and he does—by unhooking Holly's Rolex and letting Hans fall to his death.

Remember the theme stated in chapter one? John's own stubbornness caused the rift in his marriage, but the same stubbornness will save it. And, in an ironic twist, he does that by relieving Holly of her Rolex.

The watch is an important image from the beginning of the story, a symbol of Holly's success, as well as a symbol of everything John had lost (or was unable to provide her). By unhooking it, he saves Holly's life, but he also releases both of them from the toll that watch (and everything it stood for) took on their relationship.

The watch didn't matter. Only Holly mattered. Only their family mattered. John has grown and changed. His pride and stubbornness split them apart, but John is no longer the resentful man he was at the beginning of the story. He's the supportive hero. The empowering alpha. And now John and Holly are both free to ride off into the sunset together.

And hopefully he won't be a douche canoe the next time she gets a promotion, but we can't be certain, can we? Fortunately, we'll have many, many sequels to *Die Hard* to hash it out, but for now, we can enjoy what happens in the next and final chapter. The denouement.

20

DENOUEMENT

Denouement is a fancy French way to describe the falling action in the final chapter. The dragon has been slain. The battle has been won. The couple resolved their differences and can now walk off together into the sunset.

And you, dear writer, can pat yourself on the back for a job well done and celebrate with champagne or chocolate or both. I mean, after you finish this one final chapter.

Is it the most important chapter of the book? No. But it is the final thing your reader will experience. It's the last moment they take to savor your novel, so make it memorable, and make it satisfying.

This is when any yet-to-be-answered questions can be addressed. When you can tie things up neatly with a bow. And it's also when you get to employ the final image.

The final image should be the opposite of the opening image. A change has occurred within your character. They've learned and grown and healed their wounds and reached their goals. You want to demonstrate this change visually as you come full circle.

Do you remember in high school English when you studied essay writing, how the last paragraph is connected to the first? How your theme is stated in the first paragraph and restated in the last?

This is the same, but on a different scale, and with all the lessons learned throughout your novel incorporated into and celebrated in one final fantastic scene.

The opening image of Harry Potter was that of an abused, lonely orphan living in a cupboard under the stairs. In the final image, Harry is getting on the train to go back to the Dursley's home, but he's not the same person. He's happy, and he's found his place. His true home. He's surrounded by friends and classmates and people who love him. He's no longer alone, and although going back to that awful environment for the summer will suck, he knows it's temporary. He'll be right back at Hogwarts in the fall.

At the end of *The Hunger Games,* after both Katniss and Peeta are declared the winners, President Snow is furious. The head gamemaker, Seneca Crane, is escorted in a room containing nightlock berries and forced to commit suicide. Haymitch warns Katniss that if she wants to survive, she'll have to keep playing the game—by pretending to love Peeta. Although she cares about Peeta, and may even love him, she thinks of it as only part of the game. When Peeta grasps that, he's hurt and sad. His feelings for Katniss were genuine.

The final image of *The Hunger Games* is bittersweet. Peeta and Katniss are right back where they started, at the exact location where the reaping took place. Katniss's mom is mentally engaged and smiling. Primrose is alive and sitting on top of Gale's shoulders. Gale is still smoking hot, and he took care of Katniss's family as promised. But

Katniss and Peeta have changed. They are no longer a part of the crowd. They are separate. Different.

They lift their joined hands to the sky and the crowd cheers, but as Peeta releases Katniss's hand, we understand his pain. The games are over, but Katniss and Peeta still have roles to play. They are still being watched and every move they make will be analyzed. There is no going back to their lives before the reaping, and this new life is not at all what they anticipated. There is a deep sense this story isn't over. Not by a long shot.

Legally Blonde ends with Elle being chosen by her peers to give a speech at her law school commencement. She's introduced by Professor Stromwell, and the mutual respect between them is obvious. Elle has come a long way, and she's proven to everyone else what we've known all along—she is more than a pretty face. A lot more. And people finally take her seriously.

In *Die Hard*, the watch is the mirror image of what happened at the start of the movie. In the beginning, Ellis encouraged Holly to show John the watch to prove how out of John's league Holly was now. But, by removing the same watch at the end of the film, both Holly and John are set free. The watch is nothing. Their relationship and their family are everything.

Of course, since *Die Hard* is a thriller, they can't make it easy on the viewer. So, even after John unhooks Holly's super symbolic Rolex and Hans plummets to his death and we think Holly and John are safe and will ride off into the sunset together, something else happens. Something unexpected.

We were sure the bad guy Karl (aka ballet star Alexander Godunov) is dead, but he somehow rises with a gun and is about to kill John. Al (our pep talk-giving side-kick) saves him. It's a great way to end Al's character arc as well, and, at last, John and Holly can ride off into the sunset together...in the back of the limousine driven by Ajax.

Perfection.

AFTERWORD

You did it. You plotted like a boss and wrote a wonderful book. You told your story in a way that kept your reader interested and engaged, and you deserve a huge pat on the back and a giant glass of champagne.

But before you pop the cork, there is one more thing you need to know. As stated earlier, not every system works for every book or every writer. You have to find the one that works best for you. Don't feel compelled to follow my guidelines mark for mark. Even I don't follow them precisely—and this is my plotting method!

Be flexible. Think things through. But, most importantly, tell your story.

Here is the most critical advice I can give you: Only you can write the tale bubbling around inside you. Even if you're doing something you feel has been done a gazillion times, it has not been done by you. You are special. Unique. Valuable. And your story is as well.

Another thing I'd like to mention is how I came up with some of the ideas in this book. I'd love to give credit where credit is due, but sometimes you absorb things without realizing exactly where they came from.

No one lives in a vacuum. It took lots of books (by some very clever authors) and classes (by amazing presenters) to come up with this system. I wish I could give a big shout out to every single person who taught me about plotting, but that would be impossible. It's an ongoing process. I listened, learned, read, absorbed, and attempted to apply it to my own books. A piece here. An idea there. A thought or a seed planted in my mind by someone else that sprang to life and grew.

So, what I'm trying to say is I'm sorry if I learned something from a certain source and didn't give it credit. It was unintentional. But, if you're interested in seeing some of the resources I've used over the years, here is a list:

Save the Cat! Writes a Novel by Blake Snyder

Take Your Pants Off by Libbie Hawker

Romancing the Beat by Gwen Hayes

On Writing by Stephen King

How I Write by Janet Evanovich

So You Want to Write by Brenda Ueland

Derek Murphy's excellent videos and resources in *https://www.creativindie.com*

And thank you, dear writer, for the stories you tell and the way you tell them.

Now, it's time. No excuses and no fear. Your book is going to be incredible, so put your bottom in your chair, pants, or no pants, and get it done.

PLOT SUMMARY

ACT I

Chapter One:
SOMETHING HAPPENS
(Opening Image, Set-up, Theme, Catalyst)

Chapter Two:
A REACTION TO WHAT HAPPENED
(Debate occurs)

Chapter Three:
TRYING TO PRETEND IT DIDN'T HAPPEN
(Ostrich moment)

Chapter Four:
NO MORE PRETENDING
(No going back, first plot point)

Chapter Five:

MAKING A DECISION

(Breaking through to ACT II)

ACT II

Chapter Six:

FRIENDS AND ENEMIES

(B Story)

Chapter Seven:

FUN AND GAMES

(Promise of the premise)

Chapter Eight:

PROVING THEY ARE WORTHY

(First battle)

Chapter Nine:

STAKES ARE RAISED

(Antagonist revealed—or red herring)

Chapter Ten:

TRUTH AND ULTIMATUM

(Midpoint of the story, victim to warrior)

Chapter Eleven:

MAN/WOMAN IN THE MIRROR

(Protagonist sees that they have changed)

Chapter Twelve:

MAKING A PLAN
(Second battle, crucial role)

Chapter Thirteen:
OOPS. WE'RE SCREWED
(Bad guys are getting closer)

Chapter Fourteen:
UH, OH. WE'RE SUPER SCREWED
(Second plot point, all is lost)

Chapter Fifteen:
DARK NIGHT OF THE SOUL
(Rock bottom)

Chapter Sixteen:
PEP TALK
(Usually connected to the B Story)

ACT III

Chapter Seventeen:
IT'S ON
(Final battle)

Chapter Eighteen:
PLOT TWIST
(It's over, the protagonist has lost)

Chapter Nineteen:
SURPRISE WIN

(Climax, unexpected victory, theme has come full circle,
everything in the story comes together)

Chapter Twenty:
DENOUEMENT
(Falling action, and final image)

ACKNOWLEDGMENTS

A big thank you to my editor, Lara Parker, and my wonderful proofreaders, Maria Thomas and Gwen Jones. I'd also like to thank my beautiful beta readers: Denise Weaver, Robin Webster, Deborah Cantonese, Joni Neilson, Pat Perrier, Fran Colley, Diana Lynn Hunter, Melanie Mamakos, Toni Celeste, Darla Defrancesco, Vickie Fisher, Kristina Kunz, Carol Silvas, and Anne Tiller. And a final thank you to West Virginia Writers, Inc. They invited me to teach a workshop on this subject at their annual conference, and that is how this book baby was born.

ABOUT THE AUTHOR

Abigail Drake is the award-winning author of seventeen novels, but she didn't start her career in writing. She majored in Japanese and economics in college, and spent years traveling the world, collecting stories wherever she visited. She collected a husband from Istanbul on her travels, too, and he happens to be her favorite souvenir.

Abigail is a coffee addict, a puppy wrangler, and the mother of three adult sons. To learn more about Abigail, please visit her website: https://www.abigaildrake.com

ALSO BY ABIGAIL DRAKE

For more about Abigail, visit her website:

https://abigaildrake.com